This book belongs to:

_____

Bailey Comes Home

Written, Illustrated, and Photography by:

Debra Addison Steffens

Lucky 13 Publishing books may be ordered through booksellers.

Debbie Steffens P. O. Box 366 Plains, Texas

www.debbiesteffens.com

1 (806) 456-7147

ISBN: 978-1-7337359-8-8 (sc)

ISBN: 978-1-7337359-9-5 (e)

Library of Congress Control Number: 2020914273

Lucky 13 Publishing rev. date: 11/15/2020

Dedicated to my sweet precious student, Bailey Howard, who was taken from us far too soon. I miss you, my angel. Also, to all those family and friends, that prayed, visited, and checked on me during all those months in the hospital. I am blessed by your love, kindness, prayers, and God's healing hands. God is great.

As the sun rose into the sky, its rays fell upon Bailey's face. She slowly opened her eyes. It was going to be another hot and lonely day.

Bailey had been alone and wandering for most of her life. Her previous owners had left her on the side of the road. They were moving and they couldn't take her to their new home. There just wouldn't be enough room for her. She would never understand why someone would buy a puppy and not realize that it would grow up.

Even though her owners had betrayed and deserted her, she still believed, in her heart, that there were good people. She believed that someday she would find a home that loved her just the way she was. That had been her prayer every night, before she fell asleep.

Bailey was a Great Pyrenees, which meant she was a large dog. Her breed had guarded and protected herds of sheep, cattle, and goats since the beginning. She had a lot of thick, long white hair. She also had a light grey mask on her face and ears, and a black spot on her large shaggy tail.

Bailey slowly stood up, stretched, and shook off the leaves that were stuck to her coat. Her stomach growled and rumbled. She hadn't eaten in several days. Bailey began her daily search for a home. Soon she came to a farmhouse.

An elderly woman was working in her garden, hoeing weeds. Bailey began wagging her tail and walked slowly toward the woman. Finally, the woman noticed Bailey. She told Bailey to stay back, because she was afraid that Bailey might knock her down. Bailey hung her head sadly and lay down.

Just then, the woman's son drove up. He patted Bailey and scratched her ears. He gave Bailey a bowl of water. He knew someone that had dogs like Bailey. He called the man and asked him if he would like to pick Bailey up. The friend said he would take Bailey, and he came to get her. He could tell that Bailey was a sweet dog, and he said he would take care of her, even though he really didn't need another large dog.

When they got to his house, he gave her some food, and left her to meet his dogs. Now his dogs did not want any new dogs hanging around. His dogs let Bailey know that very quickly. Bailey hung her head and when no one was watching, she sadly walked away.

One of his dogs, named Duke, felt bad about the way they had acted. He followed Bailey across the field of cotton. He finally caught up with her and told her how bad he felt. He even offered to walk her to the next farmhouse.

When Bailey and Duke got there, they were very thirsty. It was hot that day. A woman and her daughter were outside cleaning their garage. They watered the dogs, but they had no dog food. They liked Bailey, but they thought that she belonged to a neighbor. So, they called him to come and get his dogs.

When they got back to his farm, Duke told the others that they had been wrong to have acted the way they had when they first met Bailey. He told them that they needed to apologize.

They all told her that they were sorry and Bailey, being the sweet dog that she was, accepted their apologies. They tried to make her feel at home and welcome. But, deep in her heart, Bailey knew that this wasn't where she was meant to be.

Early the next morning, Bailey decided to continue to explore the area. She went past one house, but the children threw rocks at her and chased her away. So, Bailey kept walking and searching. The next house had a dog in the backyard that barked a friendly hello. Bailey stopped at the fence to visit.

The dog's name was Smokey and had lived there for many years. Bailey told him how lucky he was to have a forever home like that. Smokey asked where her home was, and she sadly said she didn't have a home. Smokey was a kind dog with a big heart, so he asked her to stay. He told her that his people weren't there, at that moment, but they would be back soon.

Bailey told him thank you,but she decided to try the next house down the road. When she got there, she met a friendly little dog named Scruff.

He invited her to the garage and shared his food with her. Scruff was a very kind little dog, and he even told her about his little boy that lived there. He asked Bailey to come back the next day and see his little boy. Bailey decided that this might be a good thing to do.

Bailey dropped by the next day and met the little boy. His name was Caleb and he liked Bailey. He petted her and let her play with him and Scruff. Bailey enjoyed the game of chase and really liked playing with the little boy.

After they were tired from running and playing so hard, Bailey and Scruff lay down in the shade of a tree to rest. The little boy lay down as well, using Bailey for a soft, cuddly pillow.

Unfortunately, the parents didn't want Bailey hanging around and eating their dog's food. They chased her away. Bailey stopped back by to say goodbye to Smokey and she saw his people. The lady petted her and talked kindly to her before she went into the house.

Thinking that Bailey belonged to the man down the road, the lady called him to let him know that his dog was at her house. The man explained to the lady that she wasn't his dog and that she didn't want to be at his house. The lady loved animals and she had a big heart. This gave the lady a chance to see if Bailey just might want to stay there. The next day, the lady looked out and saw Bailey asleep on the porch. She brought out pans of food and water. She called Bailey to her. Bailey had had so many bad things happen to her that this show of kindness caught her by surprise. Bailey slowly came closer to the lady and saw the pans.

She saw the kind look on the lady's face and saw her hold out her hand. This time, the hand was offered to Bailey in friendship. The hand wasn't waving her away or holding a rock. Bailey carefully edged closer. All the while, the lady kept talking softly and soothingly. Bailey could tell that this person was different.

When she reached the woman, the lady began rubbing Bailey's ears and stroking her head. Bailey heard the kind words and saw the food and water. Big tears began to fill Bailey's eyes. Bailey's heart was so full that she began to cry and whine.

She took her foot and tried to pet the lady's foot. She leaned against the lady and continued to cry tears of joy. The lady got down on her knees and put her arms around Bailey's neck. The lady gave Bailey a big hug and told her that she wanted Bailey to know that she could stay if she wanted to. The lady told her that she had a home now. She ate and drank in between her tears. That night, with a full stomach and a full heart, Bailey slept on the porch next to the door that the lady had used.

It had been so long since anyone had really shown her any kindness. She had always believed it could happen, and she had always prayed that it would happen, that someone kind would want her. The next day, and the next, the lady would come out and feed and water Bailey and pet her. There was always water and food any time she wanted. One day, the lady brought new collars home. Smokey got a turquoise collar and Bailey had a bright pink one. She was so proud of her new collar.

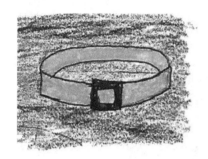

The man came home one afternoon with another doghouse, this one he built just for Bailey. It was even bigger than Smokey's house.

Bailey loved roaming the fields with Smokey. They both enjoyed chasing the rabbits that lived out back of the barn. Bailey and Smokey grew to be best friends. Smokey taught Bailey how to be a guard dog. They were extra careful if the lady was home by herself. They both lay in the front of the house, just in front of the BEWARE OF DOG sign. This was to let passersby know to stay away.

Bailey and Smokey liked to bark at the livestock in the pens out back. One of their favorite things was to play tag with the kitties and run them up a tree. When they were tired, they lay on the porch.

While they slept and rested, the kitties came and rested on the porch with them. Booger, Bailey's favorite, lay on top of Bailey.

Smokey and Bailey were very close. They spent many happy years together. One day Smokey came home and had been hurt very badly. The people took Smokey to the Veterinarian and in a very quiet room in the arms of both his people, he crossed the rainbow bridge into heaven, where he would hurt no more. In heaven, Smokey would be able to run like he had when he was young. He no longer hurt.

Even though everyone was very sad and missed Smokey badly, they knew he was in a better place.

The loss of Smokey really hurt Bailey's heart, and she was very sad and lonely. When she thought about Smokey, she wanted to cry. She had never lost anyone that special to her. The kitties knew this, so they doubled up and played with her to make Bailey feel better and less sad and lonely. In time, the hurt gradually went away and only the wonderful memories that Bailey and Smokey had shared together remained.

Those memories made Bailey smile and feel like Smokey was still close by.

One day, Bailey saw her people loading their suitcases into the pickup. She knew that they would be gone for several days. Her lady filled her large pan with her favorite dry food and topped it off with Bailey's favorite canned food. The lady told Bailey who would be taking care of her and the kittens while she was away.

A couple of days later, the man came home alone. He unloaded everything. Then he started to walk back to the pickup, he turned to Bailey and said that the lady was very sick and was in the hospital. The man seemed very sad and worried. He had tears in his eyes as he drove away. This scared Bailey. Bailey knew that this was very serious.

The lady was the one that had welcomed her to her new home. Bailey told the kitties and they were worried about the lady, too.

They all prayed she would be alright and come home soon. Day after day, week after week, and month after month, the man kept telling Bailey and the kitties that the lady was getting better.

He either fed them every day or had someone else do it do it for him, while he was with the lady at the hospital.

One day the man left yet again, and Bailey watched as the truck finally vanished from sight. Bailey sadly lay down in front of the house. Finally, she drifted off to sleep.

Bailey dreamed about running in the fields of cotton and chasing rabbits with Smokey, playing chase with the lady, and the little treats she always brought home, just for her.Bailey wondered if she was going to ever see her lady again or if she would go away like Smokey had.

The next day, Bailey saw the red pickup coming down the road. For some reason, the pickup looked happy, as it came closer.

Then, to her surprise, she saw two people in the truck. Could it be? Could it really be her lady? Bailey started jumping for joy and dancing in front of the house. It was! It was her lady. Bailey ran to the back of the house to greet her.

When the man opened the door, he told Bailey that she must be very careful with her lady, because she wasn't completely well. Bailey could hardly contain herself. She was so happy and so excited to have her lady home again. Bailey did act calm and careful as she said hello. She licked her lady's hand and was amazed that even though her lady had been so sick, she remembered to bring her a special treat.

Tears filled Bailey's eyes as well as the lady's, as she stroked Bailey's head. Bailey put her front feet on the running board of the pickup and the lady lay her head on Bailey's. The lady told Bailey how much she had missed her, how much she loved Bailey, and how glad she was to be back home.

Bailey looked at the lady and licked the tears off her face, and the lady hugged Bailey around the neck and buried her face in Bailey's soft fur.

Then Bailey jumped, bounced,and ran for the joy of having her lady home again at last.The lady laughed and clapped her hands. After Bailey had finished greeting her lady, she ran to tell the kitties that their lady was back home.

Everyone was so glad to have her home. Bailey was so happy to know that her home was again complete. The lady had to walk a lot to build up her strength. Bailey walked every day with the lady, to keep a watch on her and keep her safe. Bailey felt like she was in heaven.

Finally, her faith and prayers of a forever home had been answered. Bailey had truly come home.

Other Books by Debra Addison Steffens

The Adventures of Shadow, the Almost Black Kitten

Shadow's Utah Adventure

Smokey Finds His Wag

Shadow Visits the Alamo

CPSIA information can be obtained
at www.ICGtesting.com
Printed in the USA
BVHW022109301222
655321BV00011B/349